The "Reason Why" Books

FIBERS

Irving and Ruth Adler

The John Day Company   New York

The "Reason Why" Books
by Irving and Ruth Adler

AIR
ATOMS AND MOLECULES
COAL
COMMUNICATION
THE CALENDAR
DIRECTIONS AND ANGLES
EVOLUTION
FIBERS
HEAT
HOUSES
INSECTS
IRRIGATION: CHANGING DESERTS TO GARDENS
LEARNING ABOUT STEEL THROUGH THE STORY OF A NAIL
MACHINES
MAGNETS
NUMBERS OLD AND NEW
NUMERALS: NEW DRESSES FOR OLD NUMBERS
OCEANS
RIVERS
SETS
SHADOWS
STORMS
TASTE, TOUCH AND SMELL
THE EARTH'S CRUST
THINGS THAT SPIN
TREE PRODUCTS
WHY? A BOOK OF REASONS
WHY AND HOW? A SECOND BOOK OF REASONS
YOUR EARS
YOUR EYES

© 1964 by Irving and Ruth Adler

All rights reserved. This book, or parts thereof, must not be reproduced in any form without permission. Published by The John Day Company, Inc., 62 West 45th Street, New York 36, N.Y., and simultaneously in Canada by Longmans Canada Limited, Toronto.

Library of Congress Catalogue Card Number: 64-12332

MANUFACTURED IN THE UNITED STATES OF AMERICA

Fifth Impression

Contents

Fibers

This is a book about *fibers* (FY-burrs). A fiber is anything that is long and thin like a piece of thread. There are many different kinds of fibers. In this book we shall talk only about fibers from which people make things.

You use things made of fibers all day long, every day.

You sleep on a mattress that has a *cotton* cover. Your sheets and pillowcases are made of cotton, too. Cotton is a fiber.

The chair in your room is covered with a fabric made of *nylon, rayon, wool,* or cotton. Nylon, rayon and wool are fibers, too.

Your rug is made of wool, nylon, cotton or *acrylic* (uh-KRILL-ik). Acrylic is a fiber. Your rug may have a back made of

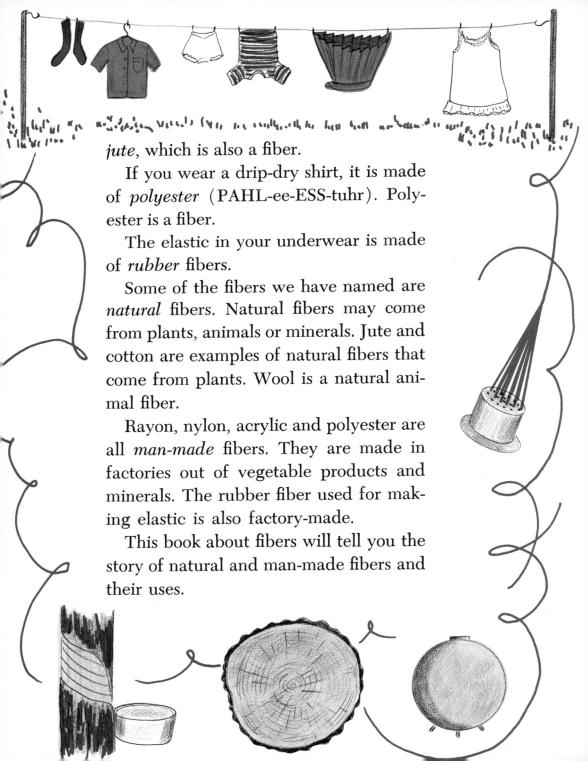

jute, which is also a fiber.

If you wear a drip-dry shirt, it is made of *polyester* (PAHL-ee-ESS-tuhr). Polyester is a fiber.

The elastic in your underwear is made of *rubber* fibers.

Some of the fibers we have named are *natural* fibers. Natural fibers may come from plants, animals or minerals. Jute and cotton are examples of natural fibers that come from plants. Wool is a natural animal fiber.

Rayon, nylon, acrylic and polyester are all *man-made* fibers. They are made in factories out of vegetable products and minerals. The rubber fiber used for making elastic is also factory-made.

This book about fibers will tell you the story of natural and man-made fibers and their uses.

Flax, a Fiber for Cloth

Flax is a fiber plant. It belongs to the family of plants called *Linum* (LY-num), from which *linen,* the thread and cloth made from flax fiber, gets its name. Flax was grown in Egypt as long as seven thousand years ago. The ancient Egyptians made rope and cloth from linen yarn.

Flax is a *bast* (BASST) or *soft fiber.* Bast fibers come from the stems of certain plants. They are found right underneath the bark. Flax fiber comes from the stem of the flax plant.

Flax grows best in places that are not too hot and not too cold. The most important flax-growing countries today are the Soviet Union, the countries in Europe along the Baltic Sea, Holland, Ireland, Belgium and France. The plants are harvested before their seeds ripen. Then the stems are not very woody and it is easier to separate the fibers from the woody parts of the stems. The plants are usually harvested by pulling them up by hand.

After the flax is harvested, the leaves and seeds of the plants are removed. The stems are tied into bundles and soaked in water. The soaking or *retting* makes the woody parts of the stem rot. In some places flax is retted in the water of lakes and rivers. In places where the dew is very heavy, the bundles are spread out on the grass to be *dew-retted.* Then the bundles of stems are dried in the sun or in special drying ovens.

6

The dried stems are now put through a machine called a *breaker*. The breaker breaks up the rotted woody parts of the stem into small pieces. Next the stems are *scutched*. Scutching removes all the wood from the stems, leaving pure flax fibers. Last, the flax fibers are *combed*. Combing removes tangled and broken fibers. The tangled, broken fibers, called *tow* (TOE), are used as a stuffing material and for making rope.

The combed flax is a light yellow fiber between 8 and 20 inches long. It is one of the strongest natural fibers. It is now ready to be spun into linen yarn and woven into linen cloth.

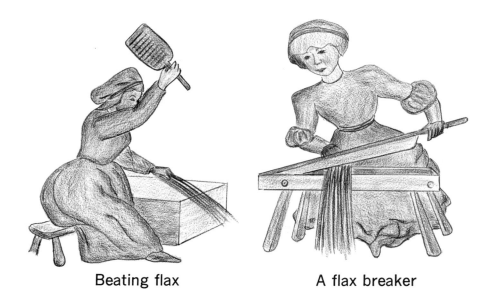

Beating flax   A flax breaker

How flax was prepared about 400 years ago

Other Bast Fibers

Hemp was first grown in Asia about 2,500 years ago. Now it grows all over the world. It is a sturdy plant that is anywhere from 3 to 20 feet tall.

Hemp fibers are prepared in the same way as flax fibers are. They are very strong. So hemp is used for making straps and canvas. It is also used for making rope. Hemp ropes are used at sea because they stay strong even when they are wet.

Ramie (RAM-ee) was first grown in China, so it is also called *China grass*. Now it is grown in many other countries. In the United States it is grown in Florida. Ramie has stalks that are 8 or 10 feet tall. Ramie stalks are put through great crushing machines which break up their woody centers. This frees their bast fibers.

Ramie is the longest of the bast fibers. Cloth made from ramie fibers is light and strong. Overalls and canvas shoes are made from it. Ramie is also used for making twine, shoelaces, and cord for fishing nets.

Most *jute* is grown in India. The plants are from 6 to 12 feet tall. Jute fiber is freed from the stem of the jute plant by retting.

Jute is a coarse fiber. So, before they are spun and woven, jute fibers are crushed to make them softer.

Jute loses its strength quickly. But it is very cheap. So it is used for making bags and sacks. It is also made into a cheap rope. A coarse, rough cloth called *burlap* is usually made from jute yarn.

Kenaf (kuh-NAFF), *roselle* (row-ZELL) and *aramina* (AA-ruh-MEE-na) are all bast fiber plants. Their fibers are sometimes used in place of jute. Most kenaf comes from India. Most roselle comes from Asia and the islands east of Asia. Most aramina is grown in Africa.

Retted jute on its way to market

9

Spinning

If you look at a single flax fiber under a microscope, you would find that the fiber is not smooth. It has bumps and holes on its surface that make the surface rough. When fibers are twisted together, their rough surfaces make them stick together to form a strong thread. *Spinning* is the way many weak, short fibers are twisted together to form a strong, unbroken yarn.

A long time ago spinning was done by hand, using a

Spinning with a spindle and distaff about 500 years ago

spindle (SPIN-duhl) and a *distaff* (DISS-taff). The combed fiber was kept in the distaff. The spinner slowly pulled the fibers from the distaff with her left hand, twisting them in one direction as she did so. She hooked the twisted fibers to the spindle which hung straight down as she worked. With her right hand she set the spindle spinning in the opposite direction. These two motions in opposite directions twisted the fibers into a tight yarn that did not unwind.

As more fiber was twisted into yarn, the spindle dropped lower and lower. When the spindle reached the floor, the spinner unhooked the yarn she had just spun and wound it up on the spindle. Then she hooked the yarn to the spindle again and started spinning once more.

This is the way spinning was done until about seven hundred years ago, when the spinning wheel was invented in India. In a spinning wheel, a big wheel is attached to the spindle by a belt. When the big wheel turns once, the spindle turns many times. So turning the big wheel makes the spindle turn very fast. The earliest spinning wheels first spun and then wound, just like a hand spinner. Then the spinning wheel was improved so that it could spin and wind the yarn at the same time.

Modern spinning machines, operated by one person, spin and wind hundreds of spools of yarn at the same time. You can read about them on page 22.

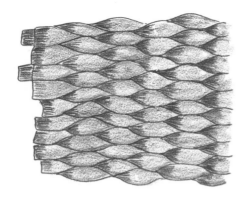

The people who lived in Egypt about 5000 years ago wove mats like this out of reeds.

Weaving

Weaving is a way of putting thin strips or threads together to make a broad, flat sheet. Thousands of years ago people know how to weave mats and baskets out of reeds and stems. They wove the stem of the flax plant, because it was strong and bent easily. When they learned how to separate the flax fiber from the rest of the stem and spin it into linen yarn, they began to weave the yarn, too. The linen cloth they wove was soft and very strong. It could be sewn easily. So, for a long time, linen was the most important cloth people made. It was used for making sails and for making clothing.

Weaving is done on a *loom*. Using a small, simple hand-loom, like the one in the picture, you can learn how to weave. First, you string threads between the notches of the loom. These threads are called the *warp* (WAWRP). The loom holds the warp threads in place, side by side. Then you weave cross threads over and under the warp

12

threads. The cross threads are called the *weft* (WEHFT) or *woof*. To make it easier to put the weft over and under the warp, you can wind the weft around a stick. Then you pass the stick over and under the warp threads pulling the weft thread along behind it. After you have passed the stick over and under all of the warp threads in one direction, you pass it back again in the opposite direction. Because the stick goes back and forth across the warp, it is called a *shuttle*. You will find that weaving on a handloom like this is very slow work.

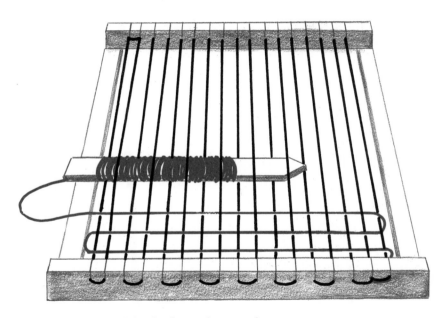

The black threads are the warp.
The brown threads are the weft or woof.

Handlooms were improved by setting them in frames that stood on the floor. By using foot pedals, the weaver

A frame handloom used about 500 years ago

could automatically raise some of the warp threads, making a space or *shed* that separated them from the rest of the warp. Then the shuttle could be passed from one side of the loom to the other more quickly than by using the over and under method. Weaving was made even faster when the *flying shuttle* was invented in 1733. By pulling on a tightened cord that was attached to the shuttle, the weaver shot the shuttle through the shed very fast. Weaving with a flying shuttle became so fast that the handspinners could not keep up with the looms.

Looms can weave many different patterns. This is done by picking different warp threads to be raised. The drawings on this page show how three different patterns can be made.

Handlooms are still used sometimes for making cloth, blankets and rugs. Most weaving today is done on large power looms that work automatically.

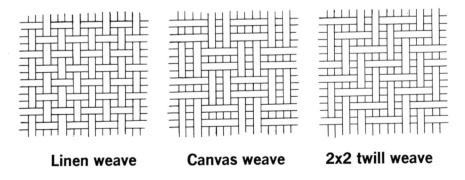

Linen weave   **Canvas weave**   **2x2 twill weave**

Some Other Plant Fibers

Sisal (SY-suhl) is a hard fiber. Hard fibers come from the leaves and stalks of certain plants. Hard fibers are not really harder than the bast or soft fibers, but they are thicker and stiffer. Sisal comes from the leaves of the *agave* (uh-GAH-vee) plant. Most sisal comes from Mexico, Brazil, Indonesia and East Africa.

Sisal is used for making rope and twine. It is woven into mats and braided into rugs.

Abaca (AB-uh-KAH) belongs to the same family of plants as the banana. The fiber comes from the tall stem of the abaca leaf. The most important use of abaca is for ropemaking. Abaca rope is very strong and very light. It is even stronger than hemp rope.

Abaca is sometimes called *Manila hemp*. This name is wrong for two reasons. Abaca is not hemp. Although abaca grows in the Philippine Islands, it does not grow near the city of Manila.

Coir (KOY-uhr) is a coconut fiber. It is made from the hairy outside covering or *husk* of the coconut.

Coir fibers are spun into yarn and woven into cloth or twisted into rope. Coir ropes cannot be used in fresh water, because they rot in fresh water. However, salt water makes coir ropes stronger. So they are used at sea.

Kapok (KAY-pock) is the white fluff found in the seed pods of the silk-cotton tree. The fibers are too short to be woven. They are used as a material for stuffing mattresses, furniture, pillows and sleeping bags.

Raffia (RAF-ee-uh) is a fiber that comes from the leaves of an African palm tree. It is used for making baskets and straw hats.

Esparto (eh-SPART-o) is the fiber from esparto grass. Esparto grass grows in Spain and Algeria. Esparto is used for making rope. It is woven into shoes and baskets.

Smashing a coconut against an iron bar to remove its husk. Coir is made from the hairy husk.

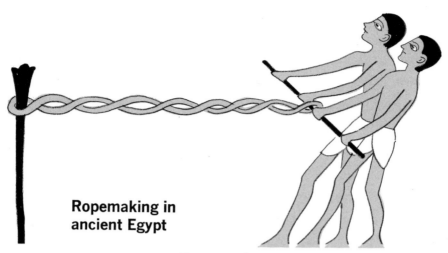

Ropemaking in ancient Egypt

Ropemaking

Stone Age men who lived more than 10,000 years ago used rope for fishing. They made rope by twisting together hair, strips of leather or natural fibers. The first Egyptians made rope from hair, flax, esparto and palm-leaf fibers. Rope was important in the lives of people who lived a long time ago. They had no machines for pulling or lifting. Ropes helped many men work together to pull or raise heavy loads.

Until 1850 rope was made by hand. Twisting a long rope took up a lot of space. So long sheds, called *rope walks*, were built in which the rope twisting was done. Some rope walks were 900 feet long.

Ropemaking machines can make ropes even miles long in a small space. Here is how ropemaking, or *rope laying*, is done.

First the fiber, which is usually sisal, hemp or abaca,

is spun into strands and wound on reels. The reeled strands are called *readies.* Three or four readies are fed into a metal block at one end of the ropemaking machine. Before the readies go into the machine, each strand is given a little bit of a twist in one direction. Then, when the readies pass through the block, they are twisted together in the opposite direction. These two twists in opposite directions keep the rope from untwisting. The finished rope is wound on reels at the other end of the machine.

Cables are made of three or four ropes in the same way that ropes are made of three or four strands.

Cotton

The early history of cotton is a big riddle. The people who lived in Peru four thousand years ago grew cotton and knew how to spin cotton yarn and weave it into cloth. Mummy wrappings found in ancient tombs in Peru are made of cotton cloth. The people who lived in India at about the same time also knew how to grow, spin and weave cotton. The cotton plant grown in America today seems to be related to a wild cotton plant growing in America and to the Indian cotton plant, too. This makes some scientists think that Indian cotton plants were brought to Peru in some way thousands of years ago. How this happened is the big riddle.

**Unopened boll
showing locks**

 Opened boll

Cotton was not used in Egypt and Europe until about twenty-five hundred years ago. Now the world uses more cotton than any other fiber. Cotton is cheap, light and strong. It is easy to spin, weave and dye. Cotton cloth has many uses. It is used a lot for clothing, sheets and towels because it can be washed easily. Cotton absorbs water. So cotton cloth is especially good for summer clothing, because it absorbs perspiration.

Most of the world's cotton is grown in the United States, the Soviet Union, China, India, Egypt and Brazil. Cotton grows in warm climates. In the United States cotton is raised in the states of the South. These states make up the *cotton belt* of the United States.

Cotton fiber comes from the seed pod or *boll* (BOLE) of the cotton plant. The cotton plant is a flowering bush. Some kinds of cotton grow to be 6 feet tall. Other kinds are only a foot tall. Different kinds of cotton have different colored blossoms. The blossoms may be white, yellow, pink or red.

The blossoms of the cotton plant last only about a day. Then the boll begins to form. The boll is divided into four or five parts called *locks*. Each lock has about nine seeds in it. Each seed has a thick mat of hair around it. These hairs are the cotton fibers. The seeds ripen about 50 days after the plant blossoms. Then the boll opens and the cotton fibers of the locks can be seen. The open boll looks like cotton candy. When the fibers have dried, the locks are removed from the bolls. This is called *cotton picking*. Most cotton picking is done by hand. It is hard work. In some places picking is now done by machine.

The picked cotton is taken to the *cotton gin* (JIN). The gin is a machine that removes the cotton seeds. After ginning, the cotton is pressed and tied into *bales* and sent to spinning mills.

Cotton fibers are much shorter than linen fibers. Most cotton fibers are between ⅞ and 1½ inches long. Even though cotton fibers are so short, they can be spun easily into a tightly twisted yarn because the fiber itself has a

Cotton fibers as they look under a microscope. Notice the twists

natural twist. Each fiber has from 200 to 300 twists.

The very best cotton has fibers between 1½ inches and 2 inches long. Cotton with long fibers is called *long-staple* (STAY-puhl) cotton. Long-staple cotton comes from Sea Island in Georgia, from Imperial Valley in California and from Egypt. Cloth woven from long-staple cotton is fine and silky.

The Cotton Spinning Mill

When the bales of cotton are opened at the spinning mill, a little cotton from many different bales is fed into a machine called an *opener*. The machine fluffs the cotton and mixes together cotton from different bales. The mixing makes all the cotton that leaves the opener about the same.

The cotton is then blown through pipes to the *picker*. The picker cleans the cotton by beating it. From the picker, the cotton goes to the *card*. The card cleans the fibers some more and makes them lie side by side. The *combing machine* finishes the job of cleaning and straightening out the fibers. The fibers leave the combing machine as a soft, untwisted rope called *sliver* (SLYV-uhr). The sliver then goes on to the *drawing frame*. The drawing frame has a series of rollers that pull the sliver, making it thinner and more even. The *slubber* finishes what the drawing frame began. It also gives the sliver its first twist. When the fiber leaves the slubber, it is called *roving* (ROHV-ing). The roving goes on to other machines which twist and pull it some more. Finally the roving goes to the *spinning frame* which gives the roving its last pull and twist. The fiber leaves the spinning frame as cotton yarn.

Cotton thread is made by twisting together yarns in the same way as cable is made by twisting together ropes.

Cotton thread must still go through a few more steps before it is wound on spools to be sold in stores.

Most thread for sewing is *mercerized* (MUHR-sirized). The thread is mercerized by soaking it in a chemical called *lye*. After the soaking each fiber is like a smooth round tube. The smoothness makes the fibers re-

Using a modern spinning frame

flect light. So mercerized fibers look shiny. The round-ness makes the fibers stronger. The mercerized thread is then *bleached* to make it snow white. Then the thread is *dyed* to color it.

Yarn that is woven into cloth usually is first dyed. The dyed yarn is wound on hundreds of spools. The yarn from these spools is then wound onto a huge 4-foot spool, called a *beam*. The yarn on the beam has hundreds of loose ends, one for each of the spools that was wound onto it. The beam is now ready to be placed in a power loom, where each loose end becomes a warp thread for weaving. Mercerizing is done after the cloth has been woven. Sometimes cloth is dyed or printed after it is woven, too.

Winding yarn onto a beam

A wool fiber looks scaly under a microscope . . .

. . . but hair does not

Wool, an Animal Fiber

Wool is the hairlike covering that grows on the skin of some *mammals* (MAM-uhls). Mammals are animals that feed their young on mother's milk. Most wool comes from sheep. Some wool comes from goats, llamas, vicuñas, camels and alpacas. The wool of the cashmere goat and of the llama, vicuña, camel and alpaca is much softer than the wool of sheep.

Although wool grows from the skin of animals the way hair does, wool and hair are quite different. Wool is scaly and hair is not. The outside of a wool fiber is made up of many tiny scales. The scales can be seen with the help of a microscope. Wool fibers are very curly, so wool is stretchier than hair. The scaliness and curliness of wool fibers make them stick together when they are twisted. This is why wool can be spun very easily into yarn. The scaliness helps wool do something that no other animal fiber can do naturally. Wool can *felt*. You can read about felt on pages 30 and 31.

25

Shearing a sheep with electric clippers

We get sheep's wool by cutting off or *shearing* the coat or *fleece* of sheep. Shearing is done once or twice a year. It is usually done with electric clippers. The fleece of grown sheep is removed in one piece. The clipped fleeces are placed on a special table where the dirty part of the fleece is cut away. This is called *skirting*. Then the wool is sorted. Sorting separates the fine fibers from the coarse ones. It separates the long fibers from the short ones. The sorted wool is baled and sent to woolen mills.

When the bales are opened at the mill, the wool first goes through a *duster*. The duster removes dust and dirt and fluffs the wool. Then the wool is *scoured* (SKOW-erd) in a chemical bath to clean it some more and to remove the natural animal oil from the fibers. The scoured wool is dried in a steam-heated oven. After scouring, the wool is still a tangle of fibers. The fibers are untangled and made to lie side by side and then twisted into wool yarn in almost the same way as cotton fibers are. (See page 22.)

There are two main kinds of wool yarn. One kind is called *worsted* (WOOS-tid). The other kind is *woolen yarn*. Worsted yarn is made from long-staple wool fibers. It is made from fibers that have been both carded and combed. So worsted cloth is smooth and can be tightly woven. Woolen yarn comes from short-staple fibers that have been carded but not combed. So woolen cloth is fluffier and stretchier than worsted cloth. Blankets and winter clothing are often made of woolen cloth. The fluffiness of woolen cloth makes it trap air and the trapped air helps keep you warm.

Knitting

On page 12 you read how to weave cloth from yarn. *Knitting* is another way of making cloth from yarn. Knitting, however, has been done only for a few hundred years. Although it is not an old craft, knitting is related to a kind of knitting that was done three thousand years ago by the people who lived in Peru and by the people who lived in Norway and Sweden.

In knitting, first a chain of loops called *stitches* is made. Then new stitches are made by pulling new loops through the old ones. Flat cloth is made with two knitting needles. As the knitter works, stitches are moved from one needle to the other and back again. Hand-knit sweaters are usually made in this way. Some knitting is done by going round and round in one direction. This

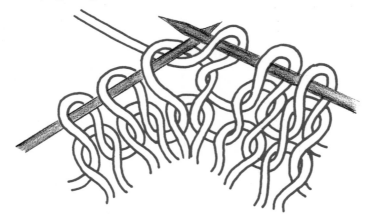

In knitting, new stitches are made by pulling new loops through the old ones.

is done using several needles with points at both ends. Circular knitting frames can be used for doing this kind of knitting, too. Socks are usually knitted by going round and round.

Most knitting today is done on knitting machines in knitting mills. Many fancy patterns can be knitted both by hand and by machine.

You can make a simple circular knitting frame from a large spool. With a frame like this you can make a knitted cord. The pictures show you how to make a knitted cord using a spool knitting frame.

Wool is the best yarn for knitting sweaters and winter socks because of its warmth. Yarns made of man-made fibers are sometimes mixed with knitting wool to make the yarn stronger. Cotton is the best yarn for knit summer underwear.

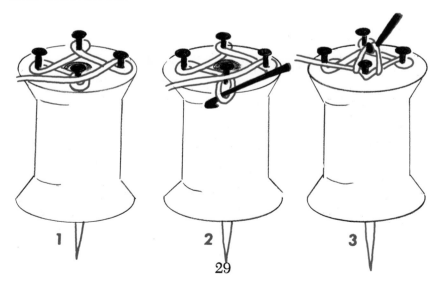

1   2   3

**Woven wool fibers . . .   . . . and felted wool fibers
as seen under a microscope**

Felt

Felt is a cloth made from fibers without weaving them
or knitting them. Felt is made from certain fibers that
are able to stick to each other when they are moistened,
rubbed, pressed and heated at the same time. The making of felt is called *felting*.

Wool is the only natural fiber that can felt naturally.
Wool felts because of its scaly surface and its curliness.
Hair can felt, too, if it is changed by chemicals so that it
acts like wool. Other fibers can felt if a little bit of wool
is mixed with them.

Felt has been made for more than three thousand
years. It has been made by machine only since 1820. In
making felt, wools of different staple lengths are mixed

together and carded. The wool leaves the carding machine as a wide thin *web*. Many webs are placed one on top of the other to form a *batt*. The batt is placed between wet cloths and steamed. Then the batt is placed between the heavy metal plates of a *hardening machine*. The plates of the hardener jiggle, rubbing the batt and pressing it. The pressing and jiggling of the hot, wet batt makes its fibers stick together so that they form a tight mat. The tight mat is felt.

Good wool felt is used for making hats, coats and skirts.

Silk

On page 10 you learned that one reason fibers are spun is because they are short. Spinning makes a long, unbroken thread out of many short fibers. All the natural fibers you have read about so far must be spun for this reason. Only silk is different. Silk usually does not have to be spun to form a long, unbroken thread because it is *naturally* a long, unbroken thread.

Silk making began in China about 4,000 years ago. However, for 2,500 years the Chinese kept the way silk was made a secret. Silk was very expensive. Kings and other rich people in Europe wanted silk. So Chinese silk had to be carried thousands of miles to Europe to supply the rich people of Europe with the silk they wanted. The

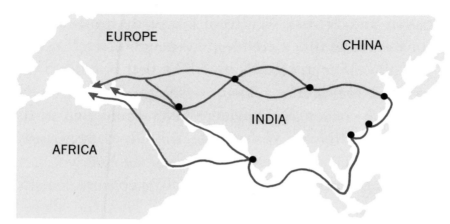

The brown lines show the routes the silk traders took

map on this page shows the path traders followed to bring Chinese silk to Europe. When people in Europe learned the secret of silk making about 1,500 years ago, they began to make their own silk. Italy is the most important silk-making country in Europe today.

Silk is made by the *silkworm*, the caterpillar of a large white moth. When the eggs of the silk moths hatch into caterpillars, the tiny caterpillars are placed on wide shelves or trays in a warm room. They are fed the leaves of the mulberry tree. The silkworms eat and eat and get bigger and bigger. After about six weeks they stop eating. Then each silkworm builds itself a little hammock on the shelf out of bits of straw that have been placed there. Once inside the hammock, the silkworm begins to wrap itself up in silken threads. In this way it spins a *cocoon*

32

(kuh-KOON) of silk. The silk is made inside the body of the silkworm. It comes out through a small opening, called a *spinneret* (SPIN-uh-RET), that is under the silkworm's mouth. The silkworm changes to a silk moth inside the cocoon. This change takes about two or three weeks. At the end of that time, the silk moth is ready to break the cocoon open and begin to lay eggs.

When a silk moth comes out of its cocoon, the silk of the cocoon is broken in many places. Then the silk of the cocoon is no longer a long, unbroken thread. To keep this from happening, most of the cocoons are gathered while the silk moths are still inside. These cocoons are put into boiling water. This kills the silk moth and helps loosen

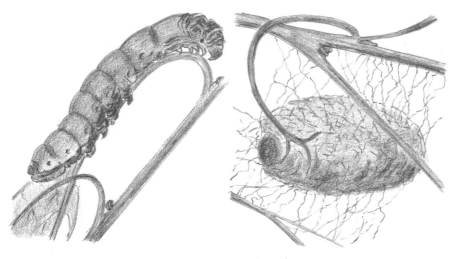

A silk worm . . .   **. . . and its cocoon**

the silk threads of the cocoon. Then the unbroken silk thread or *filament* (FILL-uh-ment) is unwound from the cocoon and wound on a reel. Several filaments are twisted together when the silk is reeled, because one filament by itself is too fine to be used as thread for sewing or yarn for weaving. Reeled silk is called *raw silk*. Raw silk is made into silk thead and woven into silk cloth.

Some of the strongest and finest cocoons are not put into boiling water. The silk moths are allowed to break out of these cocoons, damaging the cocoons. These silk moths then lay eggs which hatch into new silkworms. These cocoons and other damaged cocoons are also used for making silk thread and silk yarn. The broken silk fibers are combed and spun in the same way as cotton and wool. Silk prepared in this way is called *spun silk.*

In the past, most silk was used for making cloth for

Unwinding silk from cocoons and winding it on a reel about 600 years ago

dresses and for making fine stockings for women. However, stockings of the man-made fiber, *nylon*, have taken the place of silk stockings. Nylon and other man-made fibers have taken the place of silk in clothmaking, too. Some silk cloth is still made. But the world uses half as much silk now as it used in 1940. It uses 300 times as much cotton now as it does silk.

A Fiber from Stone

Everything in the world is made up of *molecules* (MOLL-eh-kules). A molecule is the tiniest bit of anything. Molecules are made up of *atoms* (AT-ums). A molecule of water and a molecule of salt are different because they have different atoms in them. The atoms in a particular molecule are always arranged in the same way.

The molecule of the mineral *chrysotile* (KRISS-uh-tile) has atoms of *silicon* (SILL-ih-kon) and *oxygen* (OX-ih-jen) in it, along with atoms of *calcium* (KAL-see-um) and *magnesium* (mag-NEE-zee-um). The atoms of silicon and oxygen are arranged in rings. Each ring has 6 atoms of silicon and 18 atoms of oxygen in it. The rings are held together by electrical pulls. They are held together in such a way that they form a chain. In chrysotile, the chains of rings lie side by side. Because of this, chrysotile is a fiber. Chrysotile fiber is called *asbestos* (ass-BESS-tuss), a word that means it cannot burn.

Asbestos is found in the rock, *serpentine* (SUHR-pen-teen). *Ores* with asbestos in them are broken up by explosions in order to free the asbestos fiber. After the ore has been broken up, the longest asbestos fibers are gathered by hand. These fibers are carded and combed and spun into yarn. The yarn is woven into asbestos cloth.

Because asbestos cannot burn, fire fighters often wear clothing made of asbestos cloth. People who work at other jobs at which they might get burned wear clothing made of asbestos cloth, too. The roll-up curtains used in theaters and school auditoriums are made of asbestos cloth. Then fires which may start on the stage cannot spread to the section where people sit.

Most asbestos fiber for weaving comes from Quebec, Canada.

Ore containing asbestos fibers

Man Makes His Own Fibers

During the 7,000 years that man has been using fibers, many changes have taken place. He has learned better ways to grow and harvest vegetable fibers. He has learned better ways to raise silkworms and to reel silk. He has learned better ways to raise sheep and to clip their fleece. He has invented machines for combing, spinning and weaving. With all these changes, man still used only natural fibers for spinning and weaving. Then about one hundred years ago man began to *make* fibers. Since then the man-made fiber industry has grown by leaps and bounds.

Man learned to make fibers by copying nature. At first he used natural fiber materials that he changed into a liquid. Then he copied the way the silkworm makes silk. He forced the liquid through tiny holes that are like the silkworm's spinneret. Later he began to make his own fiberlike materials. In order to make fiberlike materials, first he had to find out what the molecules of plant and animal fibers were like. He found that the molecules of all these fibers were built up of units that are all exactly the same. The units are attached together in a chainlike pattern, forming a giant molecule. These giant molecules are called *polymers* (PAHL-ih-muhrs), which means *many parts*. Man then learned the right chemicals to use

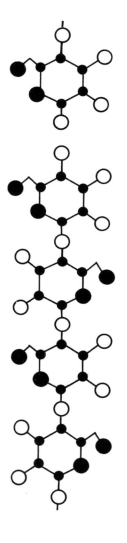

Diagram of a unit molecule of *glucose*. Glucose is a kind of sugar.

Unit molecules of glucose are attached to each other in a chain. In this way they form a giant molecule or *polymer* of flax. Flax is one kind of *cellulose*.

to make giant molecules like these. He has learned how to make many different polymers. Out of these polymers, he has made many new fibers.

Fibers from Wood

Rayon (RAY-on) is the oldest man-made fiber. It is made from *cellulose* (SELL-yeh-lohss), a polymer found only in plants. The cellulose for rayon comes from *wood pulp*. Wood pulp is wood that has been cut up and shredded. It also comes from *cotton linters,* the short fuzzy hairs that stick to cotton seeds after ginning.

The wood pulp or cotton linters are soaked in chemicals and then mashed up and rolled into great sheets of cellulose. The cellulose sheets look like huge blotters. Then the cellulose sheets are soaked in another chemical bath and crumbled up. The crumbs are mixed with still another chemical inside a large churn. The crumbs, which were white at first, are turned orange by this chemical. The orange crumbs are now mixed with a chemical which turns them into a thick liquid that looks like honey. The liquid then goes to the spinning machine where it is pushed through a spinneret with many holes. As the filaments come out of the spinneret, they pass through a chemical bath which hardens them. The final product is a cellulose filament that is called rayon.

Rayon filaments may be wound up like reeled silk and then spun into yarn. Or they may be chopped up into short lengths or staples and spun like spun silk.

Cloth made from rayon or rayon mixed with other yarns has many uses. Clothing, curtains, carpets and automobile tire linings are some of the things made from rayon.

Acetate (ASS-uh-tate) is another fiber made from cellulose. The chemicals that are used to make acetate *change* the cellulose polymers into new polymers. Acetate is made from shredded cellulose that has been

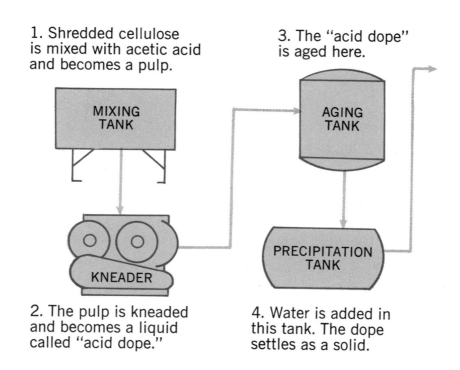

1. Shredded cellulose is mixed with acetic acid and becomes a pulp.

3. The "acid dope" is aged here.

MIXING TANK

AGING TANK

KNEADER

PRECIPITATION TANK

2. The pulp is kneaded and becomes a liquid called "acid dope."

4. Water is added in this tank. The dope settles as a solid.

changed into a liquid that can be spun. The liquid is forced downward through a spinneret into a warm spinning tube. The warm air of the spinning tube dries the filaments as they leave the spinneret. The filaments harden as they dry. Then they are twisted together to form acetate yarn.

Acetate yarn is woven or knitted into cloth for clothing.

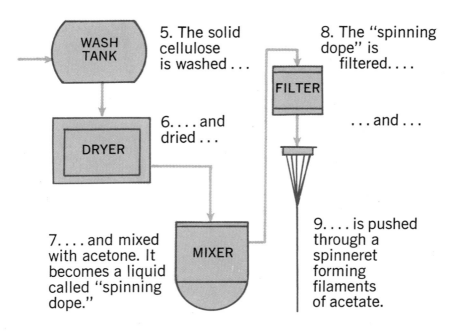

5. The solid cellulose is washed . . .

6. . . . and dried . . .

7. . . . and mixed with acetone. It becomes a liquid called "spinning dope."

8. The "spinning dope" is filtered. . . .

. . . and . . .

9. . . . is pushed through a spinneret forming filaments of acetate.

WASH TANK

DRYER

FILTER

MIXER

How acetate is made

41

A Fiber from Sap

Rubber is a polymer that is made from the milky, gummy juice of certain plants. The juice is called *latex* (LAY-tex).

Rubber is *elastic* (ee-LASS-tik). When it is stretched it returns to its original size and shape.

Rubber is manufactured by heating together latex and sulphur. It is made into a fiber by forcing liquid rubber through a small hole.

Rubber fiber cannot be woven all by itself. It may be used as the warp threads, with nylon, cotton or rayon as the weft. Or the fiber may be covered with a winding of cotton, rayon or nylon. Then the covered fibers can be used for both the warp and the weft.

Because rubber fiber is elastic, it is used to make underwear waistbands, garters and women's girdles and brassieres.

**Gathering latex
on a
rubber farm
in Java**

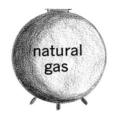

Some things that are used to make nylon

The First All Man-made Fiber

Nylon (NY-lon) was discovered by accident. Scientists were trying to find out how certain small molecules came together to form polymers. One day a chemist was taking some melted polymer out of the container in which it had been made. As he lifted it out, he found that it formed a long thread. He found that this thread could be stretched into a long, thin fiber. This long thin fiber was the first nylon filament.

Air, water and certain chemicals are used to make nylon. The chemicals are prepared from coal, oil or natural gas. They can even be prepared from corncobs or other plant products. The chemicals and water come together to form a liquid that has a nylon salt in it. This liquid is then heated in a sort of pressure cooker. Two things happen here. The water is driven off and the short molecules join up end to end, making the chainlike polymer. The polymer nylon is then pushed out, the way toothpaste is pushed out of a tube, to form polymer ribbon. The ribbon is pushed onto a cold roller where it hardens. The hardened ribbon is ground up into small flakes. Flakes from many batches are mixed together and then melted in a spinning machine. The melted nylon is pushed through a spinneret. It hardens in the air as nylon filaments. The nylon filaments are then stretched or *drawn* between rollers that turn at different speeds. Drawing makes the polymers lie side by side, in the same direction as the filament. When polymers lie side by side like this, the fiber they form is stretchy and strong. So drawing makes the nylon filament stretchy and strong. It is stronger than any natural fiber.

Single-filament nylon is used for knitting very fine stockings. Several filaments are twisted together to make yarns for many kinds of clothing. Filaments are cut into staples and spun to make heavy yarns that are used for rug making and for furniture material. Because it is so strong, nylon is used for making parachutes, ropes and auto seat belts.

Nylon that is used for ski pants, stretch socks and dancing tights is often made of *stretch nylon*. Stretch nylon is nylon that has been given a permanent wave. This is done by first twisting nylon very tightly and then heating it. The twisted nylon is then cooled, and untwisted as it cools. Next the untwisted yarn is knitted or woven into cloth. The cloth is washed in warm, soapy water. This makes the yarn in the cloth twist into millions of tiny curls, like the curls of wool fiber. When the nylon becomes curly, it shrinks, making the cloth shrink. This shrunken cloth is stretch nylon cloth. No matter how many times it is stretched, the cloth always returns to its original size and shape.

Some clothing made of nylon yarn

More and More Man-made Fibers

Fiberglas is a man-made mineral fiber made from melted glass. The melted glass is pulled through a small hole to form a filament of glass. Several filaments are twisted together to make Fiberglas yarn. The yarn is woven into cloth and dyed. Because Fiberglas cloth is really woven glass, it is not damaged by the sun. So Fiberglas cloth is used a lot for making window curtains.

Acrylic is a polymer fiber made from air, water, oil, limestone and natural gas. After the polymer is formed, it is spun the way acetate is spun. The filaments are then stretched and drawn in the same way as nylon. Acrylic is used for its warmth, the way wool is. However, it is twice as strong as wool. It is used for making sweaters, blankets, rugs and pile linings for coats.

Polyester is a polymer fiber made from coal, air, water and oil. Polyester fiber is very springy. It does not absorb water. So polyester cloth does not crush or crease easily. Wet polyester cloth dries quickly. Polyester cloth is used for making *drip-dry* clothing.

Spandex (SPAN-dex) is a polymer fiber that is stretchy like rubber. However, spandex is stronger and lighter than rubber fiber. It does not have to be covered with cotton, rayon or nylon, the way rubber fiber is, before it is woven or knitted.

Fiber Index

About the Authors

Irving and Ruth Adler have written more than fifty books about science and mathematics. Dr. Adler has been an instructor in mathematics at Columbia University and at Bennington College, and was formerly head of the mathematics department of a New York City high school. Mrs. Adler, who formerly taught mathematics, science, and art in schools in the New York area, recently also taught in Bennington. In addition to working with her husband writing this book, she drew the illustrations.

Books by Irving Adler alone and books by him in collaboration with Ruth Adler have been printed in 77 different foreign editions, in 10 languages and in 9 paperback editions.

The Adlers now live in the country in Shaftsbury Township, near Bennington, Vermont.